Welcome to the Disney Learning Programme!

Sharing a book with your child is the perfect opportunity to cuddle and enjoy the reading experience together. Research has shown that reading aloud to and with your child is one of the most important ways to prepare them for success as a reader. When you share books with each other, you help strengthen your child's reading and vocabulary skills as well as stimulate their curiosity, imagination and enthusiasm for reading.

In this book, Sofia and Amber make costumes for a fancy dress ball. But when Amber tries to compete with her sister for the best costume, she learns that sharing with the people you love can be the best prize of all. You can enhance the reading experience by talking to your child about a time when they shared a treasure with friends or family. How did sharing make the experience more fun? Children find it easier to understand what they read when they can connect it with their own personal experiences.

Children learn in different ways and at different speeds, but they all require a supportive environment to nurture a lifelong love of books, reading and learning. The *Adventures in Reading* books are carefully levelled to present new challenges to developing readers. They are filled with familiar and fun characters from the wonderful world of Disney to make the learning experience comfortable, positive and enjoyable.

Enjoy your reading adventure together!

© 2015 Disney Enterprises, Inc. All rights reserved.

Scholastic Children's Books
Euston House,
24 Eversholt Street,
London NW1 1DB, UK

A division of Scholastic Ltd
London • New York • Toronto • Sydney • Auckland
Mexico City • New Delhi • Hong Kong

This book was first published in the United States in 2013
by Disney Press, an imprint of Disney Book Group.
Published in Australia in 2014 by Scholastic Australia.
This edition published in the UK by Scholastic Ltd in 2015.

ISBN 978 1 4071 6296 6

Printed in Malaysia

2 4 6 8 10 9 7 5 3 1

Papers used by Scholastic Children's Books are made from woods grown in sustainable forests.

www.scholastic.co.uk

The Fancy Dress Ball

ADVENTURES IN READING

By Lisa Ann Marsoli

Illustrated by Character Building Studio
and the Disney Storybook Artists

King Roland and Queen Miranda
are going to have a ball!
It is a fancy dress ball.

Everyone will make a costume. There will be prizes for the best costumes.

Amber wants to win first prize.
'I will be a peacock,' she says.

'You will be a pretty peacock,' says Sofia. 'I will be a fairy princess.'

Amber tries to make her costume.
Feathers go everywhere!

She is sad. Her
costume does
not look good.

Amber goes to Sofia. 'I cannot make my costume,' she says.

Sofia looks at Amber's drawing.
'I can help you,' she says.

Sofia sews feathers onto Amber's dress.
She makes Amber a feather cap.

Amber loves her new costume!

Then Sofia makes her own costume.
There is a frilly pink skirt.

There are sparkly wings.
There is a crown of flowers.

Amber sees Sofia's costume.
It is much prettier than hers!

'I will make my costume prettier,'
says Amber. She finds more feathers.

James sees Amber in the garden.
'It is time for the ball,' he says.

Amber rushes to get feathers.
She falls over in the mud!

At the ball, everyone is having fun.

But where is Amber?

'I wanted a better costume than you,' Amber tells Sofia.

Amber is very sad.

'I have an idea,'
says Sofia.
'Let us share
my costume!'

She pulls her costume apart.

Sofia makes two frilly pink skirts.
She makes two more sparkly wings.

She makes two flower crowns.
'Now we are both fairy princesses!'
Amber says.

They go back to the ballroom.
It is time for the prizes.

The Three Good Fairies
are the judges.

Maya and Jin win a prize.
Khalid wins Best Costume.

Amber and Sofia win a prize, too.
'But my real prize is my sister!'
says Amber.

Sofia the First

Princess Lesson

A true princess knows that helping a friend is magical.